how happy is
your
Love Life?

50 Great Tips to Help You Attract
and Keep Your Perfect Partner

Sophie Keller

How Happy Is Your Love Life?
ISBN-13: 978-0-373-89249-5
© 2011 by Sophie Keller

Author photograph by Sarah Corwin Photography

Library of Congress Cataloging-in-Publication Data
Keller, Sophie.
   How happy is your love life? : 50 great tips to help you attract and
   keep your perfect partner / Sophie Keller.
       p. cm.
ISBN 978-0-373-89249-5
1. Man-woman relationships. 2. Interpersonal relations. 3. Love. I. Title.
HQ801.K443 2011
306.7--dc22
                        2011010358

How Happy Is is a trademark of Sophie Keller.

www.Harlequin.com

Printed in U.S.A.

The Fruitstock Music Festival in
Regent's Park, London, England.
Sunday, August 10, 2003,
at approximately 4:15 p.m.

This book is dedicated to my ANYWHERE,
ANYTIME, and yours to come.

CONTENTS

Introduction ix

Quiz: How Happy Is Your Love Life? 1

PART I: PREPARING FOR LOVE 11

1 Remember That the Cards Are Always Shuffling 12

2 Work on Yourself from the Inside Out 13

3 Let Go of Your Secrets 15

4 Learn from Your Past Relationships 17

5 Evaluate Your Friendships 22

6 Heal Old Family Wounds 24

7 Get Rid of Unworkable Beliefs That Prevent Success 26

8 Take the Feedback; Leave the Failure 31

9 Discover What Else You Are Good At 32

10 Recover from a Breakup Healthfully 34

11 Burn Away Your Past to Make Room for the Future 37

12 Know Exactly What You Want 38

13 Surviving the Holidays (Especially Valentine's Day) While Single 41

14 Love Yourself to Attract New Love 43

v

PART II: LOOKING FOR LOVE 45

15	Mix with People Whose Relationships Work	46
16	Look at Your Parents	47
17	Get Out of the House	49
18	Be Imaginative to Help You Find What You're Looking For	51
19	Believe in Abundance	55
20	Learn about Your Date	56
21	Don't Expect Perfection	59
22	Look for Someone Who Is Open to Change	60
23	Understand That What You See Is What You Get	62
24	Pay More Attention to Internal Qualities	64
25	Feng Shui Your Single Life	65
26	Prepare Your Bedroom for New Love	68
27	Stop Playing Hard to Get	72
28	Don't Rush into Sex	73
29	Fluff Your Feathers	76
30	Commit to Dating	77
31	Look Your Best	79
32	Make Sure That You Are on the Same Page	81
33	What NOT to Do on a First Date	83
34	What to Do on a Date	86

35	Make Small Talk	88
36	Follow These Tips for Internet Dating	91
37	Find Out These 7 Essential Things about Your Date	96

PART III: CREATING LIFELONG LOVE 99

38	Fan the Small Flame	100
39	Mind the Third Person in Your Relationship	102
40	Discover Your Sexual Compatibility	103
41	Be Clear on Money Issues	104
42	Look at a Potential Partner's Relationship History	106
43	Connect Through Vulnerability	108
44	Understand How Men and Women Communicate Differently	109
45	Praise and Appreciate Your Partner	112
46	Be a Good Listener	113
47	Avoid These 7 Red Flags	114
48	How to Recognize if They Like You	116
49	Every Cell Has to Scream, "Yes! Yes! Yes!"	117
50	Have Faith in Timing	118

| Quiz Answers: So, How Happy *Is* Your Love Life? | 120 |
| Acknowledgments | 129 |

INTRODUCTION

ANYWHERE. ANYTIME.

That is *where* you can meet your life partner, and that is *when*. Remember that when you're sitting at home grieving over a failed relationship. Remember that when you are fed up with being alone. Remember that when you feel so ready and have felt that way for so long and yet he or she refuses to appear.

You could be in a store, at a music festival, crossing the road, introduced by friends, in a library, in a class or at the gym. The possibilities of where you might meet are endless, and that, of course, is the beauty of it. And you don't know when that fateful moment might be, because meeting your partner is one of the things in life you cannot control, and it usually comes when you are least expecting it.

And on that day when you do finally walk up the aisle to meet your husband-to-be or wife-to-be, you will wonder why you wasted so much time being frightened and not trusting that one day this would happen to you when it has happened to so many people before you and will happen to so many after.

As anyone who has met his or her life partner will attest, it is usually a sliding-door moment that has as much to do with timing as it does with anything else. You need to be ready, your partner needs to be ready and then there is a third universal element that needs to be ready. However you choose to look at it, whether you believe in divine intervention, the planets aligning or pure luck, when you do meet your life partner, more often than not you will realize that the timing is perfect. Maybe six months previously you were living in another country or still in a relationship, or maybe your partner was still busy enjoying playing the field. Whatever was happening, one of the three elements was not in place and it is only in hindsight that you will see that timing is key.

Take my story, for instance.

On August 11, 2003, the Fruitstock Music Festival was taking place in Regent's Park in London. I was there that afternoon, having a picnic with my brother and some of his friends. Simultaneously, my now husband, Oliver, walked out of his house in Maida Vale to go to his mother's house for tea. As he approached his Vespa, his neighbor, Leanne, walked out of her house at exactly the same time. One minute earlier or later and they would have missed each other.

"Hi, Oli," she said. "We're going to a music festival in Regent's Park. Do you want to come with us?"

"Sorry, I can't," said Oli. "I've got to go to my mum's for tea."

"Come on," said Leanne. "Come for just half an hour. Quite a few of your old friends will be there. Nick, Charlie…"

"Okay," said Oli. "I'll come for fifteen minutes."

As I was sitting on the grass with a group of people, I saw a man in the distance, maybe fifty yards away, walking toward us. I got up, almost unconsciously, and walked toward him before he was even close.

"Hi," I said. "I'm Sophie."

"Hi," he said. "I'm Oli."

We were engaged four months later.

That is how it can happen, out of nowhere and as quickly as that. ANYWHERE. ANYTIME. One day you're single; the next you're with your life partner.

There is one final aspect to this story. Oliver and I were long distance for six months. Even though I am British, I was living in Los Angeles and he was in London. When I went back to London the following April to prepare for the wedding, we went to his aunt's house for dinner. She said, "Sophie, I have photos of you when you were a child." She went to her bookshelf and pulled out an old album, flipped through it and opened a page of photos of her daughter's birthday party, and there I was, as a baby—with Oli.

Perhaps you've met your life partner and don't know it yet, or perhaps you have yet to meet him. Maybe you've been single for what feels like ages, or maybe you're fresh out of a relationship and frustrated that you haven't met someone special yet. Maybe you are dating someone now but aren't sure if he or she is really "the one." If you can relate to any of these possibilities, then this book is for you.

Every tip in this book is designed to help you create a happier love life. The tips are designed to shift your consciousness and bring you to a place where you feel completely happy with who you are, and help you clarify who it is that you are looking for so that you can attract that person. And once you've met someone who is a possibility, there are tips to help you determine if he or she is truly the one.

All you need to do is to keep working on yourself, drop the need, get out of the house and then let magic happen, because it will. It did for me, it does for millions of others every day and it will for you. In the meantime, enjoy this book, which I hope will be a good companion on your journey, and be sure to let me know when you meet your life partner.

Love, Sophie

QUIZ: HOW HAPPY IS YOUR LOVE LIFE?

Read each question and circle the answer that best applies to you and your love life. If there are steps you can take to improve your love life based on your answers, turn to the relevant tips in the book and start creating a happier love life, one tip at a time!

Circle the answer that sounds the most accurate, then turn to page 120 for your results.

1. **When you finish a relationship, do you:**
   A. Feel an immense amount of anger toward your ex and speak critically about him to your friends and family?
   B. Brush the experience and your feelings under the carpet and try to move on as quickly as possible?
   C. Try to determine what worked and what didn't in the relationship and what you would do differently next time?

2. **What is your attitude toward finding a partner?**
   A. Some people are lucky and find their partners and others don't.
   B. There is a complete lack of eligible partners out there.

C. The world is an abundant place and there is someone out there for everyone, including me.

3. **How similar are the people you date to one or both of your parents?**
   A. I find myself attracted to people with similar negative characteristics to those of my parents.
   B. I find myself attracted to people with similar positive characteristics to those of my parents.
   C. I date people who are nothing like my parents.

4. **When you are in between relationships, do you:**
   A. Feel that you can't enjoy your single life because you are so desperate to meet your partner?
   B. Enjoy the time that you are single and do lots of great activities, as you want to make the most of it?
   C. Quite enjoy it and partake in a few new activities while you bide your time?

5. **When issues come up for you in a relationship or at the end of one, how do you deal with them?**
   A. I sweep it all under the carpet for fear of what I might find.

B. I consciously read books, go to therapy and do other self-development programs to better myself.

C. I occasionally open up to a friend.

6. **When you are dumped, do you:**

   A. Take a break from relationships to build up your courage before getting yourself back out there?

   B. Not really care, since you are thick-skinned by now, and continue dating?

   C. Vow you will never go out with anyone again?

7. **If you introduce a new partner to your family and nobody particularly warms to them, do you:**

   A. Ignore your family's opinions (after all, what do they know)?

   B. Listen and take what they say into account, although you do not let it sway you completely?

   C. Drop the relationship (after all, your family knows you best)?

8. **How important is it for you to have sexual chemistry?**

   A. Very, since I can in no way have a relationship without it.

B. If I like the person but the sex is just okay, I can put up with it.

C. So long as we get along well, I do not need much sexual fulfillment.

9. **When you are at the beginning of a relationship, how open are you with your innermost secrets?**

   A. I reveal everything without considering the consequences.

   B. I open up a bit about myself at a time, sharing more as the relationship grows.

   C. I reveal nothing for fear my partner won't like what he hears and will walk away.

10. **When it comes to the holidays and hanging out with your family, do you:**

   A. Love having time alone with your family?

   B. Get really miserable because you do not have a partner?

   C. Enjoy the time that you have with your family but wish you had someone with you?

11. **When it comes to what you are looking for in a life partner, do you:**
    A. Have no clear idea?
    B. Spend time formulating a realistic goal and you are clear about what you are looking for?
    C. Know what you don't want but you are less clear on what you do want?

12. **What is the state of the relationships of most of the people around you?**
    A. Most of my friends and family are either single or divorced.
    B. Most of my friends and family are in relationships that have their problems.
    C. Most of my friends and family are in loving, open and very communicative relationships.

13. **When it comes to going out and socializing, what best describes you?**
    A. I find social situations difficult to handle and therefore don't go out very much.
    B. I push myself to go out, and then once I am out, I really enjoy it.

C. I am very social and love going out and meeting new people.

14. **How diverse is your social life?**

    A. I always go to the same places and remain in my comfort zone.

    B. I like to try new places to have new experiences and meet new people.

    C. I sometimes go to a new place if I am persuaded to by a friend.

15. **In the early stages of dating, if your date annoys you, do you:**

    A. Dump her quickly as she doesn't meet your ideal?

    B. Put up with anything, as you are so happy that someone is interested in you?

    C. Remain flexible in your approach and give him a chance (after all, no one is going to be perfect)?

16. **Do you always attract the same kind of person with similar difficult personality traits?**

    A. Yes, there is an obvious pattern; they all have similar traits.

B. No, they are all different and there is no obvious pattern.

C. The significant ones are similar and some of the others are not.

17. **When you start dating someone and notice an obvious red flag that suggests a potential relationship is unlikely to work out in the long run, do you:**

A. Ignore the signs and still go out with the person? It's better than being alone!

B. Walk away before you get too attached?

C. Have the courage to discuss the red flag with him early on and make a decision about what to do depending on his answer?

18. **When it comes to dressing for a date, do you:**

A. Put in some effort to look nice and casual and wear something that reflects your personal style?

B. Dress to the nines and wear things that you would not normally wear just because you think he might like it?

C. Not dress up at all since he should like you au naturel (otherwise he isn't for you)?

19. **If you have a mutual attraction with someone who is in an unhappy relationship, do you:**
    A. Tell him to call you after he has finished the relationship he is in and had some time by himself?
    B. Consider this an opportunity to date him on the side and think that maybe you can help rush his decision so he can be with you?
    C. Not care if he is with someone or not, since you want to have some fun while you wait for "the one"?

20. **What are your typical dating patterns? Do you tend to:**
    A. Not go past the first date?
    B. Not last more than three months?
    C. Have a series of long relationships that end up not working out?

21. **When you are out, do you recognize the signs if someone likes you?**
    A. No, I usually have no clue.
    B. Sometimes I can read them and sometimes I can't.
    C. I can always tell.

22. When you start dating someone, do you have sex:

   A. Pretty much immediately, even on the first date, if there is a big attraction?

   B. After you've been out on a handful of dates?

   C. Once you've waited to make sure you get along well, that you both feel an emotional attachment and the relationship is going somewhere?

23. If you start dating someone you like but find out that she has money issues, do you:

   A. Drop her like a ton of bricks?

   B. Do your best to make it work if you really like her?

   C. Give her money and let her live off you?

24. How comfortable would you be if someone moved in with you?

   A. I could easily make space for someone to come and live with me.

   B. If I had to, I could get rid of some of my stuff and sacrifice some privacy but would find it hard to do.

   C. I have a lot of stuff and would rather not have to move it around or get rid of it.

25. If the person you are going out with asks you to marry him, will you:

   A. Marry because he is the only one who has asked and there are no guarantees that you will get another offer?

   B. Marry only if every cell in your body screams "Yes"?

   C. Marry because you like him, even though there are some issues, but you think he has the potential to change?

PART I

PREPARING FOR LOVE

1 Remember That the Cards Are Always Shuffling

There are nearly seven billion people on the planet and the cards are always shuffling. People are in and out of relationships all the time. No matter what your age and where you live, there is someone out there for you.

2 Work on Yourself from the Inside Out

Lao Tzu said, "Be really whole and all things will come to you."

I love to quote this because if you are truly yourself, fully and completely, then there is no doubt you will magnetize the perfect person for you. However, if you are still hiding behind masks and armor, then you are obviously going to attract people who have similar pretenses.

So work up the courage to improve yourself and do everything you can to work through any old issues that you still have left over from when you were a child. These issues can manifest themselves as unwanted behaviors or unworkable beliefs that you have copied from your parents, siblings, peers, teachers or any other parental figure in your past. Or equally they could be behaviors and beliefs that at the time were useful to adopt to help protect you from people or circumstances that made you feel unsafe.

These old behaviors may have been effective and kept you safe years ago, but they are not serving you now. In fact, they are most likely preventing you from growing and it is time to let them go. As you do so, you can discover who you really are,

what you are meant to do in your life and who you are meant to magnetize toward you. You are already whole and complete; it is now a matter of shedding masks and releasing armor so that you can express your unique, empowered and original nature—which is essential for attracting long-lasting love!

With all this in mind let's start by looking at your relationship patterns. Do you have a habit of getting involved with someone and then ending the relationship right around three months because you have a deep childhood fear of not feeling free? Perhaps you have a habit of moving too quickly, and you try to imagine your future together after the second date for fear of being abandoned, because one of your parents left or wasn't around when you were young. Or maybe you overreact when you get upset or withdraw when someone says something you don't like, because that has always been your way of coping. All these are learned patterns and ways of protecting yourself. Now is the perfect time to work on yourself to let go of these old ways so that you can reap the benefits and rewards later on by attracting a similarly open, honest and maskless person. (Like attracts like!)

3 Let Go of Your Secrets

Release the close-guarded secrets that you are terrified that someone might find out about you if they get too close. Whether it is that you are bad with money, sweat a lot, were in an unhealthy or abusive relationship or were bullied at school, you need to let these sorts of things go rather than hide them and let them eat you up.

We all have things in our past that we are embarrassed about or might feel shameful of, so don't think you are alone. At twenty-one I was in a self-development training class where the trainees were all sitting in a circle and the trainer kept asking, "Secrets, who has secrets?" For hours we were in that room as I and the other participants stood up at various intervals and confessed secrets that we had held inside for so long for fear that if we told anyone about them, they would seem so big and shocking that that person would have a lesser opinion of us. But by keeping them close to our chests, we allowed these skeletons in the closet to eat us up. Many of us thought that we were alone in the secrets that we kept, but during this exercise we all recognized that many of us shared similar ones!

In my life coaching practice I have taught CEOs, celebrities and everyday people, and regardless of social and financial situations, I have found that we all have similar issues to varying degrees.

It's easy to try and shove things under the carpet, but they always manage to find a way to rear their heads at one point or another. The truer you can possibly be to who you really are, the greater the reward you will have with the partner that you attract.

4 Learn from Your Past Relationships

Every relationship that you are in before dating your life partner is a rehearsal. With each relationship that doesn't last, you are learning about how you behave when you are in a relationship and the unworkable patterns that you keep repeating.

Some of you may have obvious patterns. For instance, maybe you always date emotionally unavailable people or are attracted to people who are already in a committed relationship. Whatever your pattern is, it may not be apparent at first glance and you might have to be a bit of a detective to find it.

For instance, when I looked back on my relationship history, a distinct pattern emerged. I'd stay with a partner for about a few years, and in one way or another, they were emotionally unavailable. I caught one boyfriend having secret affairs, another boyfriend withheld sex and then I dated a middle-aged man who had never been in a stable relationship before.

The fact that I kept going out with emotionally unavailable men was my issue, not theirs. Herein lay the secret to what was stopping me from getting what I wanted: an emotionally open relationship. Once I unearthed this pattern, I dug deep into my past to uncover why I was making such inappropriate choices in the present and, as a result, made some major changes in myself to let go of the issues. Then I took a break from dating so that I could make a conscious new choice in who I dated next. The work that I did paid off, and after six months of being single, I finally met someone emotionally available, Oli.

What Can You Learn from Your Past Relationships?

The questions that follow are designed to reveal any dating patterns you might have. With the insight that you glean, you can determine if you want to change your patterns of behavior to attract a different kind of mate.

When you have some quiet time to yourself, sit down comfortably with a notebook and pen and write a list of your previous partners. Next to each name write down the answers to the following questions:

1. How long did this relationship last? (Notice if there is a pattern of time that you tend to be in a relationship.)

2. Which personality traits of this partner worked for you? (For example, my ex was very good at saying sorry.)

3. Which personality traits of this partner didn't work for you? (For example, my ex was quick to get angry.)

4. During the relationship what worked in the dynamic between you? (For example, the sex was good.)

5. What didn't work in the dynamic between you? (For example, we often irritated each other and our arguments escalated and got out of control.)

6. How did you assist in the relationship not working? (For example, I made myself too available and didn't maintain my own friendships and interests enough.)

7. What were your partner's complaints about you? (For example, he said he felt I stifled him.)

Once you've answered these questions for each partner, look over the list and ask yourself the following questions:

1. If there is a common link in the dynamics of the past relationships that you have listed, what do you think it would be?

----

2. What are the similarities in the people that you have attracted?

----

3. From the information you have gleaned, what specific issues are you going to work on so that you can break your pattern of attracting similar types of people and attract someone different in the future?

----

4. From what in your past do you think the issues stem?

----

5. What are the next practical steps you are going to take to work on any issues that have emerged here?

Once you figure out your patterns, you can put time and effort toward shifting your behavior to attract someone more suitable.

5 Evaluate Your Friendships

While you are single and working on yourself to attract a different kind of partner than you have had before, it is also a great opportunity to look at the friends that surround you and who you are attracting in other areas of your life. If you notice, like in your romantic relationships, that some friendships that you have are not so good for you, then this is a good time to let go of them to make space for friendships that are more nourishing and supportive. In the same way as romantic partners, not every friend has to be in your life forever. Some friendships might last a lifetime, but others come and go depending on many different factors, such as if you and a friend are going through similar experiences. But just as a good romantic relationship grows, strengthens and evolves over time, so does a good friendship develop as the years go by.

Here's a helpful way to evaluate your current friendships: before you spend time with or speak on the phone to a friend, check how your energy feels on a scale from 1 to 10. Then once you have spoken or spent time with this friend, notice if you feel more energized or drained and again assign your energy level a number from 1 to 10. If you feel drained, then make a note of that. The next time you are with this friend, do the same thing, and make sure to note any differences in your energy level. If you do this test over a long period of time and you always feel more drained after being with this particular friend or speaking to her, then perhaps this is an outdated friendship. If you feel energized after your interaction or time together, then that is fantastic—that is a nourishing relationship.

Of course, you have to make a few exceptions for this test. If your friend is going through a really hard time for genuine reasons, then don't do the test, as you need to take her life situation into account. You don't want to put your friendship on trial if your friend is going through a rough patch.

6 Heal Old Family Wounds

When you are single and in between relationships, you should do everything you possibly can to help shift your consciousness and clear away any hang-ups you have so that you magnetize a different kind of person to you the next time around.

If there is a relationship that you want to improve in your family, whether it's with a parent, sibling or any relative who is close to you, then now is a perfect time to do it. You will often find that if you do this, inadvertently it will affect who you attract next on a love level. And trust me, the person you attract will look carefully at the dynamics within your family, so the more at peace you can be with family members, the better. Your familial relationships don't need to be perfect, but if you are working on them, it shows your future partner that you have the intelligence and drive to evolve within your relationships, rather than to remain stagnant or focus on upsets from the past. For example, if you are already in your thirties and you still blame your father for having left you when you were seven or your mother for drinking throughout your childhood, then that could signal to a potential partner that you have unfinished business and he might not find that reality attractive.

So try to work through any issues you have concerning your family when you are single and focus on how you are the master of your own destiny, regardless of what happened in your past. At some point you will want to take responsibility for your own life choices and behavior. So that you can work through what you need to, let it all go and move on.

7 Get Rid of Unworkable Beliefs That Prevent Success

Many of the limitations that you face in your love life are self-imposed, because of the negative beliefs that you may have about yourself, and how you expect others should or shouldn't behave when dating or when in a relationship. And even though beliefs have the capacity to change over time as your experiences change, many of your limiting beliefs keep you closed off and can diminish your options and stop you from getting what you want.

We adopt beliefs in the first place because they help us to grab hold of some kind of certainty in an uncertain world. So the question is, how do you uncover what negative beliefs may be preventing you from moving forward?

If you listen to your internal voice over a period of time, you will be able to uncover some of the more prominent negative beliefs to which you unconsciously adhere. They may have been passed down from a sibling, a parent or another adult at a time when you were most vulnerable. Or you may have just decided from your own past experience that certain things are true and you haven't updated those opinions over

26

time—which leaves no space for the fact that they may not be true anymore!

When it comes to your relationships, you really must become acutely aware of what you are saying to yourself. You want to stay away from unworkable beliefs or generalizations, such as:

I am not good enough to be in a long-term relationship.

Nobody will want to marry me.

I'm better off alone.

None of my relationships ever work.

I'm too much for anyone to handle.

Men don't want to commit.

Women always want to tie me down.

Do any of these false beliefs hit home for you, or do you have your own to add to the mix? Your unworkable beliefs may not initially be that obvious to you, but it is important to figure them out as they are part of what stops you from attracting who you want. If you want to meet someone, then you need to have beliefs that empower you and keep you persevering and moving forward without giving up.

By completing the following exercise, you will uncover the negative beliefs that are stopping you from moving forward and getting what you want and you will simultaneously adopt new beliefs that support your progress.

Answer the following questions:

1. The three beliefs that have limited me in my dating experience are:

----

2. The three empowering beliefs that I would rather have as I date are:

----

3. The three beliefs that have limited me when I am in a relationship are:

----

4. The three beliefs that I would rather have when I am in a relationship are:

----

5. What I must do next to make my answers to 2 and 4 happen is:

_____

_____

_____

Your goal is to let go of the beliefs that limit you and develop ones that make your life more exciting, easy and successful.

8 Take the Feedback; Leave the Failure

Anyone worth her salt has a short or even long list of relationships that didn't work and has lived to tell the tale. Anyone worth her salt has been battered and bruised a bit in the past from having her heart broken at one time or another and still lives to tell the tale. These experiences, which may feel so destructive at the time, actually help you in so many ways. For starters, these past heartbreaks help you to become more compassionate and more appreciative of what you do have when you finally meet the person that is for you.

Each time you pick yourself up after having your heart broken and put yourself back out there, you are getting closer to a relationship that does work—so long as you see any mistakes you made in your last relationship as feedback for the future, not as a failure on your part. So don't ruminate on your past mistakes and don't obsess over what you could have or should have done. What is done is done and it's over. Forgive yourself for anything that you might have done that didn't work for you and see it as feedback to do something different next time and move on.

9 Discover What Else You Are Good At

So you are single and have lots of time on your hands to do what you want to do. Take my advice—don't waste it. What are the things that you have always wanted to do but either haven't had the time to do or have even been scared to do? This is the time to do those things, before you get into another relationship and have less time for yourself again. Write down a list of activities and then choose one and dare to be a beginner again, whether it's learning to swim, improving your cooking, learning to ride a horse, taking surfing lessons or a design course. Go and do it.

In between each of my relationships I would fit in so many different activities and hobbies, and then, when I was in a serious relationship and had less time, I would cut back, because I would spend more time with my boyfriend at the time. But the great thing about being so busy is that I never wasted any time and knew that all these classes and hobbies not only helped me to meet lots of new people but also made me a more interesting and diverse person.

Here is a list of a few of the things that I did in between my relationships: I trained to become a practitioner of feng shui, a professional astrologer and a yoga teacher. I learned to read tarot cards and do hand analysis. (I'm not very good at the latter!) I took a course in directing and wrote two stage plays. Then I trained as a hypnotist, and for years I studied neurolinguistic programming. I could actually go on, as the list is quite extensive, but you get the idea. Carpe diem!

Time is too precious to waste, and adding to your abilities and interests makes you a much more fascinating person. It shows how you are passionate about life and what it has to offer and that you are hungry to learn and to better yourself. Even if the other person doesn't have the same hobbies or interests as you, your desire to delve into new experiences shows that you have an interesting, multidimensional personality.

So choose something that you have always wanted to do and go for it!

10 Recover from a Breakup Healthfully

Finishing a relationship is never easy and the feelings of loss can often be very deep and painful. But this time of loss does pass. Feelings and thoughts come and go all the time, and in a few weeks, months and, in some very hard cases, years, this will all be a memory. Maybe one moment you feel angry, then you feel sad or disappointed and the next moment you feel fine. Make sure you acknowledge all the feelings that you have, rather than denying that they are there. You don't want to stifle them or hold on to any feeling in particular, as this is not good for your health. It is important to get to the root of why you feel the way you do and to work through it.

Stay in the present as much as you can and put one foot in front of the other. When you wake up in the morning, have a notebook and pen available by your bed and first thing write down five things that you are grateful for in your life. Then, throughout the day, focus 100 percent on whatever activity you are engaged in, so that you keep out of your head. If your feelings overwhelm you, then become aware of your surroundings, your breath and where you are right now. If that means that you must name five objects around you and their colors, then do that. For example, you could say, "I see a blue sweater. I see white curtains. I see a pink telephone." And then list five sounds that you hear at that moment. For example, you could say, "I hear the sound of cars. I hear the sound of people talking. I hear the sound of typing." Then focus on your body and notice what you are feeling physically. Say, "I feel the floor beneath my feet. I feel my arm on the table. I feel my lips touching each other." Then if you need to, relax your jaw, drop your shoulders and focus on your breath. Every time you feel yourself drifting off into dark thoughts, come back to what you are seeing, hearing and sensing in your physical body, and if you really want to know where you are in the present moment, look down at your feet, as where your feet are is where you are!

You may also want to give yourself a break by taking the focus away from yourself and putting it on others. A good way to get through this period and being so inwardly focused is to make a difference in other people's lives so that you also have outer focus as well. Remember, there is a big, wide world out there, with billions of people, and you don't want to fall into a black hole of isolation for too long. I have always found that when I feel low and help others, I feel better about everything.

So you might compliment someone on his tie in the supermarket, give to a homeless person, plant flowers on a street near your house where there are just weeds, volunteer at your local animal shelter or take time to read to the kids at a local daycare center. I suggest you do those activities, because giving to others will help you to heal and have a sense that you are part of something bigger, that we are all connected and there is a great life out there beyond your breakup.

No doubt when you emerge from this experience, you will be a very different person and will have learned a lot about yourself. You will have changed and grown, and when that happens, your life does get better, as you have shifted to a new level of consciousness. But to move to a new level, you often have to go underground first, in order to rise up like a phoenix out of the ashes, so to speak. This is a growing experience for you and a time of deep fundamental change, which can take you to a new level of consciousness and in many cases to new love around the corner. And if you need to seek help, don't be afraid to do that. Often an external guide or coach can be very helpful at this time.

11 Burn Away Your Past to Make Room for the Future

A good way to help you heal from a past relationship is to write a letter to your ex and not actually send it. This letter is one in which you say everything that you want and need to say, in which you let out everything that you are feeling inside. This letter you write for yourself so that you can feel better, not to actually send.

I remember doing this after I broke up with the last guy that I dated before my husband. There were things I wanted to say that he didn't really need to hear, but I needed to get them off my chest. So I chose a quiet time, put on some classical music and wrote him a vehemently angry letter. There were moments that I felt so angry, I dug the pen into the paper. But I found that a bit of letter writing actually brought up some anger I felt for other past boyfriends as well, so I included them in the letter, too. I didn't censor anything, and as my anger dropped away, I experienced sadness. Then, when I was finished, I went to the grill outside and burned the letter and, as far as I was concerned, burnt all the ties that I had to him and to all the others in the past, to allow myself to be free and to start fresh!

12 Know Exactly What You Want

Everything that you search for externally needs to be figured out internally first. So you need to be very clear and to define for yourself the kind of person you are looking for. In a notebook, do the following exercises:

A. Outline your goal

Write down specifically what you are hoping to accomplish, making sure to use positive language. For example: *My goal is to meet my life partner within two years and to be married in five years.*

Don't be concerned if you do not achieve your goal in your time frame. Just write down one goal for now and be reasonable. Your partner and the universe need to be ready as well, so just because you might be doesn't mean that they are.

B. Choose the qualities you want in a partner

List the top ten qualities you would like your partner to have.

Here are some examples:

Warm	Loving	Loyal	Risk-taking
Creative	Independent	Extroverted	Serious
Quiet	Laid-back	Funny	Childlike
Spontaneous	Driven	Intellectual	Confident
Imaginative	Enthusiastic	Introverted	Courageous
Charming	Intuitive	Open-minded	Optimistic
Organized	Perceptive	Sensitive	Reliable
Realistic	Sense of Humor	Rational	Devoted
Considerate	Adventurous	Outgoing	Happy
Friendly	Genuine	Sexy	Stable
Emotional	Sensible	Accomplished	Gentle

When you think about what sort of person might be good for you, you need to take into account your personality and how you would both fit together. If you are both always telling jokes, it could be quite tiring. If you are both always making plans, perhaps it wouldn't give you enough space to be spontaneous and take risks. Try to consider how well your qualities will work together.

C. Put these qualities in order of importance

Once you have picked out your top ten qualities, arrange them in order of importance.

D. Identify what makes each quality so important

Next to each quality, write why it's important for your future partner to have it.

For example:

Loyal—It is important for me to feel safe in the relationship, especially since I am going to make myself extremely vulnerable. I am a very loyal person and I want to make sure my partner puts the same value on this trait as I do.

Driven—I find it very sexy to be with someone who is passionate about what they do for a living and wants to strive to make things happen for himself.

Funny—I have a tendency to be quite intense and serious, and I need someone who will lighten me up and make me laugh.

Once you've identified what you want in a partner, it makes it that much simpler to go out there and find it.

13 Surviving the Holidays (Especially Valentine's Day) While Single

Valentine's Day, Thanksgiving, Christmas and Easter are all meant to be celebratory times of the year. However, for some who are single, these holidays can be extremely hard and unbearably lonely. Let's take Valentine's Day as an example to demonstrate some ways to get over the loneliness of the holidays. You can then apply these ideas to any other time of the year when you need a shift in perspective.

1. In one way or another we have been hypnotized into thinking that February 14 is a really important date. But please do remember that even though Valentine's Day is an old, classic, established tradition, it is also a highly commercialized occasion that vendors capitalize on to sell cards, flowers, chocolates and other gifts, and that restaurants use as an excuse to charge outrageous prices for set menus. Not very romantic when you dissect it, is it?

2. If you prefer to take Valentine's Day seriously, then try to change your perspective and view Valentine's Day as a universal day of love, which is actually a much healthier approach.

That means it becomes a day to remind you to love yourself, your family, your friends, your associates and human beings in general. That's something we can all celebrate!

3. If you are concerned that last year you were with someone and this year you're single, don't be. Just be aware that it is better to be by yourself and to wait for the right person to come along than to celebrate a day with someone who isn't right for you, just so that you can fill in a hole and feel that you are not alone.

4. If you are single now, enjoy it. When you do meet the person for you, you will have plenty of Valentine's together, and many people who are together choose not to take the day too seriously. In a relationship that works well, every day presents the opportunity to give love to your partner, and there is no need to make just one day out of 365 days an extra special one.

5. Let this be a day for you to think about what kind of relationship you do want and let it serve to remind you of what qualities you are looking for in a partner. Take time to write down again what you are looking for on any particular day when you feel you need a bit of a boost. Believe me, it really can help lift your spirits!

14 Love Yourself to Attract New Love

As you become more whole and accepting of yourself and who you are, your power to attract a mate goes up. This is because the more self-assured you are, the more attractive you become. People who are self-confident tend to have an aura about them that is really appealing. It is a presence that cannot be easily defined.

If you look at the word *presence* and deconstruct it, it becomes *pre essence.* Underneath the masks and armor that you have created is your "essence," and the more you do to peel back the layers of armor and take off your old, unworkable masks, the more your "essence" will show. Authenticity is very appealing. And with authenticity comes confidence, and the more confident you are, the more friendly and open you tend to be.

As you peel back the layers, you will notice over time that your body becomes freer as well, and as a result, how you sit, stand and walk changes. Your posture changes. Posture is so important in the mating process. It is so much more attractive if you walk tall and your body is naturally relaxed than if you hunch your shoulders, as if you are protecting yourself or as if you have the world on your shoulders. Posture says so much about your personality and your confidence, and having great posture and standing straight send the message that you are a confident, empowered person. If you feel that you need to work on your posture, then try doing yoga, Pilates or, more specifically, the Alexander Technique, which deals directly with your posture when you sit, stand and move. It helps you to lose the harmful habits you have built up over a lifetime of stress and teaches you to move your body in a more natural, free and empowering way.

PART II

LOOKING FOR LOVE

15 Mix with People Whose Relationships Work

No man is an island and often people go through life transformations in groups. People move in waves, and if your friends are meeting partners, then that means that you are in the ebb and flow of meeting someone special, too. You see it all the time with groups of friends: one friend in a group gets married and then it seems like everyone else ties the knot as well. Likewise, when one friend has kids, the others probably aren't too far behind.

With that wave effect in mind, if you are looking to be in a great relationship, then mix with people who are already in great partnerships so that it rubs off on you. Take stock of how happy your friends are. If you are around a lot of people who are in dysfunctional partnerships, then you need to be careful that you don't attract the same dynamic as well. If you notice that this is the case, then you might want to spend some more time with people who are in the kind of relationship that you wish to emulate.

16 Look at Your Parents

Believe it or not, your ideal partner probably has many of the same best qualities of your parents. If you are interested in men, write down the five best qualities of your father, and if you are interested in women, write down the five best qualities of your mother. (If you had only one parent or caretaker, then write down his or her best qualities, regardless of gender.) Using this list, you will get a very good indication of the kind of person that you are likely to get along very well with.

For example, my father's best qualities and my husband's are the same. They are both warm, gentle, giving and sensitive, both interact easily with others and, as my husband pointed out while I was writing this, both have a weakness for ice cream!

If, on the other hand, while you are dating, you find that you are unconsciously going for a partner who has some of your parents' best qualities but also many of their worst, that isn't such a good thing.

Let me give you an example. You are a woman and your father has a penchant for wine, so you find yourself drawn to men who have drinking or addiction problems. Or your father was always working away from home, so you go for someone who also works away from home or is in some other way "not there."

This isn't going to lead to a long-term happy relationship and you need to take steps to heal your parental relationships so that you stop attracting partners with the same unworkable qualities.

17 Get Out of the House

Although it is appealing, you are never going to meet your future partner while sitting at home, eating ice cream and watching your favorite reality show! No, you need to get out there, mingle with other single people and play the dating game.

It's like a raffle. If you don't enter, you can't win. Which means that you need to go to places that you don't usually go to in order to see new people and be seen. There is no point in thinking that you'll meet someone at your neighborhood bar if you've already been going there for years and haven't yet met anyone who is the slightest bit suitable.

You need to get out of your comfort zone and go to some places that you haven't been to before. You can even start some new hobbies. Think about where the type of person you are looking for might go. I met two long-term ex-boyfriends in yoga classes. Maybe you'll meet your partner in a running club or a cooking class or through a volunteer opportunity.

So write a list of five places that you haven't been to before where you think you might be able to meet the kind of person that you are looking for.

Here are some examples:

A music festival

A tennis club

A dog park

A cool new restaurant

The gym

An art gallery opening

5 New Places I Could Visit

Then put time aside, dress accordingly, and go out and have a good time!

18 Be Imaginative to Help You Find What You're Looking For

I have fire walked three times. When you learn to fire walk, you are taught to rely on your three major senses (sight, touch, hearing), filling your mind with images, feelings and sounds so that you are otherwise engaged when you walk across the burning hot coals and you don't burn your feet! Here are a few clues on how to do it:

Sight—Keep your eyes up and never look down at the burning coals.

Touch—Do a movement with your arms before you start and continue with it as you walk across the burning coals to engage your feeling sense.

Hearing—Choose a mantra and repeat it as you walk across the coals.

I don't mean to say that meeting your future partner is exactly like walking across hot coals (although I am sure we have all been on plenty of dates where it felt exactly like that), but when you are looking for a mate, you need to direct your senses wholeheartedly toward what you are going to see, feel and hear when you meet him.

Answer these questions:

1. **What will you see to let you know that you have met your life partner?** Imagine it now in your mind's eye.

    For example:

    I am going to see my life partner proposing to me.

    I am going to see my life partner waiting for me as I walk down the aisle.

    I am going to see myself in the mirror in a wedding dress or a tuxedo before I get married.

2. **What are you going to feel that will let you know that you have met your life partner?** Imagine feeling it.

    For example:

    I am going to feel completely loved.

    I am going to feel safe.

    I am going to feel that I have come home.

3. **What are you going to hear to let you know that you have met your life partner?** Imagine hearing it.

   For example:
   I am going to hear him say, "Will you marry me?" or "I want to spend the rest of my life with you."

   I am going to hear her say, "I am in love with you."

   I am going to hear her introduce me to others as her fiancé.

Take a few minutes to close your eyes and really imagine how it would feel to have all three of those feelings. You want to show your body how it feels to experience those feelings.

Keep practicing. Once you have done this, you want to keep creating this feeling for yourself at any spare opportunity that feels right to you. Practice when you are lying in bed, have a moment to daydream in a doctor's office or are even waiting for a bus! This way you will know when it happens, as you have already experienced the feelings so many times inside that you are really clear about how it is going to feel when you do meet your future partner.

When I met Oli, I knew he was the one on our first date because I had the feelings of complete safety and familiarity that I had practiced so many times. It was a beautiful, boiling hot summer's day in London and he picked me up on his Vespa.

I had just passed my motorbike test and so I was exceptionally impressed when he turned up with his Vespa. And just a few days before his mother had said to him, "You'll never find a nice girl if you don't have a car!"

First we went to Notting Hill for lunch and then we walked around Portobello Road Market, where Oli pretended we were married to a tarot reader. (And he claims it took him a few weeks to know!) Then we jumped back on his Vespa and we rode around all the amazing sights of London: the Houses of Parliament, London Bridge, the London Eye, Tate Modern, the Tower of London, the Dome. You name it, we drove past it. As he drove, I held on tight to him, and by the time we got to the Dome, I started to recognize that I was having the feelings that I had created from doing this exercise. All I can say is that I felt that I had "come home." I whispered in Oli's ear, "I am so happy right now." His whole body went from being slouched to straightening up, like his soul lifted, and I had an inkling that he felt the same way.

19 Believe in Abundance

I come from the perspective that the world is an abundant place, and I strongly believe that if you want to make your life work, then you need to have the attitude that there is enough to go around for everyone. There is enough money, there is enough work, there are enough friends and, above all, there is enough love! If you adopt that perspective, you will always have more than enough of all the above.

Even in those rare moments in my life when I nearly lost hope that I would meet someone special, hearing about two people getting engaged or married, or seeing a fantastic, loving couple together, was always an inspiration and kept me moving forward and believing that there was someone for me. It proved that it does happen. If it was possible for them, then it was going to be possible for me and it *is* possible for you.

If you energetically want to attract someone to you, then give to others and wish your friends and family well who find their partners before you find yours. If they find what they are looking for, it means that you can easily be next and find what you are looking for as well.

20 Learn about Your Date

When you start dating someone you like, a good way to get to know him a little better is to ask him a few questions so that you get a really good idea of who he is. I have listed a few fun questions you might want to ask. You could always make an evening of it and go out for dinner. Bring this book and ask each other the questions or perhaps pick a few and focus on those. By doing this, you can share a little bit about each other and have fun doing it.

Once you have more knowledge about each other and it's clear that the relationship is developing, take some time to get to know your date even better. You might want to browse through his preferred websites, read one of his favorite books, watch one of his most beloved movies, learn more about his work or take an interest in one of his hobbies, without needing to necessarily take it up yourself. The more you know about who you are dating and the more he knows about you, the closer he is going to feel to you and you to him, and he is going to be thrilled that you made the effort to jump into his world a bit.

1. What would you say is your biggest passion in life?

2. What would you say you are best at?

3. Which household chore do you enjoy doing the most?

4. What is your favorite way of relaxing?

5. What were you happiest doing as a child?

6. What are your three favorite bands?

7. If you had to move to another country, where would you want to live?

8. If you had to choose a definitive three-course meal for yourself, what would you choose to eat?

9. What is your least favorite food?

10. What are your three best character traits?

11. What is your worst character trait?

12. What animal do you most identify with?

13. What cause are you most passionate about?

14. Who are the three famous people, dead or alive, that you would like to have as dinner party guests?

15. What subject interests you the most, and wish you knew more about?

16. What are your three favorite books?

17. What were your favorite subjects at school?

18. If you were to write a book, what would the genre be and what would it be about?

19. What is your worst habit?

20. What makes you a good friend?

21. What are your three favorite internet sites?

22. What do you value most in life?

23. What difficult experience in your life has made you a stronger person?

24. What do you most admire about your parents?

25. What do you believe that you are here on the planet to do?

21 Don't Expect Perfection

One surefire way to stay single is to fantasize about meeting the perfect person and not commit to anyone else in the meantime. You imagine meeting and marrying someone as cute and as funny as the Cameron Diaz character in *There's Something About Mary* or someone as macho yet sensitive as Russell Crowe's character in *Gladiator* and you're willing to hold out until he or she turns up. But these people don't exist in real life, and waiting for them to appear will keep you from forming a relationship that does work in the real world. In short, waiting for the "perfect" person who has every positive quality known to humankind will mean waiting alone, perhaps indefinitely. So be realistic. Remember that what you are looking for is not a fantasy figure, but a real human with a mélange of realistic qualities.

22 Look for Someone Who Is Open to Change

One of the most important traits to look for in a partner is an openness to growing and developing as a person, rather than a resistance to change. If you choose to be with someone who is resistant to change, you will find that you will still grow and transform over time but he won't. And this will ultimately lead to the two of you becoming incompatible. You don't have to grow at the same rate, but you both need to be making changes. If one of you is transforming and healing old wounds and the other opts not to, then the relationship might not last.

A really healthy relationship is one where you are both open to growing and transforming and you have a mutual desire to support each other and give each other the space to become older and wiser together. In this way, you will have the honor of watching and supporting your partner's transformation, while your partner will get to experience the same opportunity with you. Signs of someone open to change include:

He can easily say "I'm sorry."

She is not stuck on being "right" all of the time.

He accepts feedback easily and makes changes
if necessary.

And, of course, just as you are looking for someone who is open to change, you need to be open to change yourself, as possessing that attractive quality will make you that much more appealing to potential partners!

23 Understand That What You See Is What You Get

One very common mistake you can make is to fall in love with a person's potential, rather than who he is right now. Remember, there are no guarantees that another person is going to want to change in the way that you envision for him. You might think that he would be better off if he changed, but he may not agree. So if you like someone, like him for who he is now, rather than who you think he could possibly be at his best.

For instance, I think my husband has the body structure to be really toned and athletic-looking, and I think it would be lovely for me to feel a six-pack stomach every day! But at the moment he doesn't have the desire to do what it takes to have one. And knowing him, he probably thinks I have the potential to be a really good cook if I put my mind to it. But the truth is I just have no interest. Not right now, anyway! And we accept each other for who we are right now.

Years ago one of my boyfriends asked me to marry him, but I felt that he was not as sexual as I was and it would be hard for us to spend the rest of our lives together and for me to feel unfulfilled in that way. I thought, *If only...I could make this relationship more passionate, it would be perfect.* We both tried everything to make it work—sexy underwear, vitamins, tantric workshops. You name it, we tried it. I was so convinced that passion was the only element that was missing in an otherwise great relationship (which, by the way, is rarely the case, as your sexuality is an expression of your mental and emotional connection). In many ways I was like Cinderella's sister trying to make the shoe fit.

Now I see how futile those attempts were. It took me three frustrating years to figure it out! So my advice is to love your boyfriend or girlfriend for who he or she is now, and if you are incompatible in a way that is a deal breaker for you, then don't think that he or she can change—what you see tends to be what you get!

24 Pay More Attention to Internal Qualities

When you think about choosing a life partner, don't rely on glistening external qualities. If you have in your mind that you want someone who is rich, good-looking and very athletic, you might get that, but generally speaking, these qualities are more transient than others. You really want your focus to be on other, more sustainable qualities, such as how loyal, warm and generous a person is.

External qualities may make you temporarily happy on the outside, but they will not make you happy on the inside over the long run. If those are your priority, then you might find that you end up very lonely in your relationship. So pick what is really sustainable and important to you on the inside. You will hopefully have a long life ahead with your partner, one filled with joy and adventure, as well as many challenges. Ideally, you want someone who will stand by your side through thick and thin.

25 Feng Shui Your Single Life

The closest object to you outside of your own body is your home. Your home layout really reflects who you are, how you express yourself in the world and what you need to work on.

Feng shui translates to "wind and water," and it is an ancient Chinese practice that was developed over three thousand years ago. It involves the flow of chi (energy or life force) throughout the house and the art of placing objects so that energy flows freely and steadily into all areas of your home.

Here are some tips to help you create a sense of balance and harmony within your home so that you can attract someone new and special into your life.

Clear It Out

If you have just ended a relationship or you haven't had one for a while, you need to clear out your whole house, every part of it—every corner, every drawer and every wardrobe. If you haven't worn an item of clothing in the past six months, or in the past year at the most, get rid of it. If there are trinkets you no longer need or books you are never going to read again, then give them away to someone who may need them more than you or sell them.

As you are clearing things out, imagine that you are doing this to make space for someone else's belongings. The clutter that you have keeps you locked in the past, and if you are overloaded with stuff, you will find it difficult to move forward in your life.

Don't just dump what you don't need in your garage, as your garage is also part of your home and has an influence on you. In fact, when I work with clients and go to their homes to help transform and improve the energy there, I always take a look in the garage, because however much someone has straightened up for me, the garage invariably gets neglected. It is akin to the unconscious mind, where I can find out what is really going on!

Fix It Up

Once you have completed the clearing-out stage, your focus needs to move to step two, fixing everything that needs fixing, such as a broken window, a stiff lock, a leaking tap, a creaking door or a missing latch. You want to repair your home, as well as yourself, so there is no leaking energy! As you do this step, imagine healing old wounds and imagine feeling more whole than you have ever felt before.

Clean It Up

Make sure that all your windows are clean, as dirty windows indicate that you can't see clearly. Clean your house from top to bottom.

Once you have cleaned your house, if it needs a fresh coat of paint, then go for it. If it doesn't, then simply wash the walls with a mixture of water and nine drops of lavender or citrus oil in a bucket to clear away the dead energy from the past.

26 Prepare Your Bedroom for New Love

Once you've cleaned your house, it's time to give your bedroom a feng shui makeover. Here's how:

Tranquility

Your bedroom needs to be a place of complete calm. It is the one area in your house that is reserved for sex and sleep. If you have any electronics in your room, clear them out. Also, you don't want to have too many books in there, just the few that you are reading.

The Bed

Make sure that your bed is inviting and big enough for two, and if you still own a single bed, consider an upgrade. However, if you are buying a new bed, I suggest a queen-size bed over a king, as it will prove to be better for your sex life! In America, king-size beds have a split box spring at the bottom, which creates a psychological split. If you already have a king-size bed, then put a large red sheet between your box spring and mattress, symbolically drawing them together, and then imagine having lots of sex!

Also, it is best that only the head of the bed is flush against the wall. If the long side is against the wall, it is impossible for two people to get in and out easily.

Make sure you have two sets of pillows, two side tables and two reading lamps. Put a fresh flower or flowers on the side of the bed that you are inviting the person to, to help draw in new energy, or place a plant there, which symbolizes new growth.

Pictures and Photos

It's a little obvious, but do remember to take all photos of your former lovers down, especially in the bedroom! And while you're at it, remove any photos of family members from your bedroom. It is not very romantic having your mother, brother or grandma staring at you while you are having sex! You also do not want any photos of you alone in the bedroom, or around the house, for that matter! The images in your bedroom must add to the sense of calm that you are creating in there, so if you have pictures up in your bedroom, make sure that they are relaxing to look at.

No Pets in the Bed

Sorry pet lovers! But most beds are for two, and if your dog or cat sleeps with you, there is hardly room for one more. Some of you may protest that you have a king bed and there is more than enough room. But psychologically there is not, and when you bring a date back to your house he might find it really off-putting to go out with someone who sleeps with a pet. Subconsciously, it can potentially give the underlying message that you already have a partner. Ideally, you want to retrain your pet to sleep in another room. However, if you really can't survive without your cat or dog in the bedroom, then make a bed for her on the floor.

Bedroom Location

Imagine your front door as the front of the house and draw a line between the front and the back of the house. The best place for a bedroom is at the back of the house, behind the midline. Usually most of the activity is at the front of the house. The back is where it is more serene and quiet and also where you will naturally feel more safe and secure. It is really the ideal location for your bedroom.

Bed Location

You want your bed to be in the commanding position in the room, which means that you want to make sure that you have the widest possible view of the room, with a clear view of the bedroom doorway, without being in line with the doorway, so that you are not hit by fast-moving chi while you are in bed. At the same time you want to make sure that your bed is not under a window as that will affect the quality of your sleep. Make sure that your bed has a headboard, which is firmly placed up against the wall. If you have trouble seeing the bedroom door when lying in bed, then put a mirror up opposite the door so that you can easily see if someone is coming in without turning your head. This will help you to sleep better, which will lead to a clearer mind. And that is exactly what you need in looking for your next romantic partner!

Once you have made all the changes that you intend to make, try this: Shut your bedroom door and stand on the outside of it. Close your eyes and relax completely. Imagine that you are a visitor about to see your bedroom for the first time. Open your eyes and open your door. Take note when looking inside your bedroom of whether you feel relaxed or stimulated. Does the room feel cozy or cold? What is your overall impression of the room? Depending on how you feel, you may need to make some alterations. Now is the time. Once you have finished with all your changes, get a friend to view your bedroom and see what she feels when she sees your bedroom for the first time.

27 Stop Playing Hard to Get

Playing hard to get doesn't work if you are looking for an authentic long-term relationship as it can send the message that you are unavailable emotionally. Although it may intensify feelings of want or lust at first, in the long term playing hard to get doesn't actually increase your chance of getting (or not getting) the guy or girl. If you are meant to be with the person, you will be with them.

Looking for love is a serious business for a lot of people, and sometimes *playing* hard to get can come off like you are toying with someone and not being quite honest. By the same token, avoid people who play games with you or send you mixed signals.

28 Don't Rush into Sex

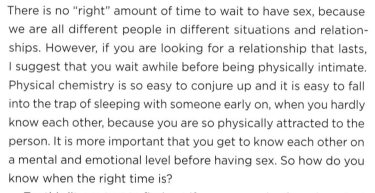

There is no "right" amount of time to wait to have sex, because we are all different people in different situations and relationships. However, if you are looking for a relationship that lasts, I suggest that you wait awhile before being physically intimate. Physical chemistry is so easy to conjure up and it is easy to fall into the trap of sleeping with someone early on, when you hardly know each other, because you are so physically attracted to the person. It is more important that you get to know each other on a mental and emotional level before having sex. So how do you know when the right time is?

Try this litmus test to find out if you are ready: If you have just started dating someone, imagine having sex with him (a nice thought I am sure!). However, then imagine how you feel after having sex with him. If you have any of the following feelings when you imagine the aftermath, then you are not ready.

Signs that you are not ready:

1. You regret being with him and you wish you had waited.

2. You feel depressed after being with him and wish you had waited.

3. You feel distanced in some way during and after sex. Or you are conscious that he feels distanced during or after. (Remember the film *When Harry Met Sally* and the shot of Harry staring at the ceiling after having sex with Sally for the first time? You know he is thinking, *What have I done, and how do I get out of here quickly!*)

4. You worry that you might have contracted an STD.

If you imagine having any of those feelings, then *wait!* Don't do it. You are not ready and could get very hurt if you have sex too soon and the relationship does not work out.

Signs that you may be ready:

1. You know a lot about him, his family and friends.

2. You both understand who each other is and you have discussed how you both feel about important topics.

3. You feel that you have a lot in common, including your values.

4. You are already in a committed monogamous relationship with each other and you feel sure the relationship has a future.

Using a litmus test is a much better way to gauge when to have sex than waiting a set amount of time. However, if you are desperate for me to give you a time frame, then see if the relationship passes the three-month mark. Often at three months you can tell if a relationship is going to continue or if a relationship is going to end. That might be roughly ten dates. If you have seen each other only twice in that time, then you might want to wait longer.

Make your own conscious decision and I mean *conscious*. Do *not* let the moment run away with you, as you will regret it later on. And if you imagine feeling any of the signs that you are not ready, then *wait*. If he is "the one," he will not be going anywhere anytime soon!

29 Fluff Your Feathers

Who isn't attracted to talent? Who isn't attracted to someone who applies her mind or has interesting hobbies? When you are on a date, don't be too modest about what you're good at or your past endeavors. All of that is really attractive. You don't need to show off, of course, but it's good to show that you excel at some things and can apply yourself.

As at a job interview, when you are on a date, there is nothing wrong with fluffing your feathers and accentuating your positive traits. Just as you use styling products to enhance your hair and you make sure that you smell nice, you can let your date know if you are good at tennis, won a poetry prize or worked in an orphanage in Africa. How you present yourself says so much about who you are.

30 Commit to Dating

When you do decide to get out there and really start dating, you need to be prepared to make an effort and really go for it. That means that you need to put in a lot of work and make space for love in your life, as it does take up time. If you are at work 24/7, you are probably not ready to seriously start dating, as there is no space for anyone or anything other than work at this moment in your life. So when you make the decision to commit to dating, go for it. Do not do it halfheartedly.

Dating should always be fun. If you go on a date and it goes really badly, it can always make a good topic of dinner party conversation to chat about with your friends. Then there are the dates where you meet someone great, but you have no sexual attraction—but maybe that person will end up being a new friend who, in turn, meets his life partner through you!

Then there are the dates where you get along quite well and are fairly attracted to each other, but for some indescribable reason things are just a bit lukewarm. Those are the most difficult ones, but they still can be fun, because there is always the chance for excitement and adventure.

By adopting the cup-half-full mentality (rather than half empty), you can actually start to see dating as a great time in your life, when you are going to meet many great people that you would not have met before. If you think about it like that, then you understand that dating is not necessarily just about finding a mate, even though that is perhaps your primary motivation. Dating is about socializing and meeting stimulating people you may otherwise have never spoken to.

If you need to take time off from dating to have a break, do so. Dating in phases can be a good idea. But don't lose faith and always remain optimistic. Know that the odds are very high of you meeting someone fantastic if you keep going out. It is often a numbers game. Keep moving forward, because you never know who is around the corner. We have all had to kiss a few (or more than a few) frogs in order to find our prince or princess. And remember that you can meet him or her. ANYWHERE. ANYTIME.

31 Look Your Best

When you start dating, make sure that you look as good as you can to increase your confidence. Go to the gym or start a new exercise regime if you have been meaning to. Get in shape, get your hair done, create a whole new look and buy clothes that fit your body type and colors that suit you. Throw out all your old, tired clothing and make sure you look really good when you go out on the actual date. Remember, less is more, but at the same time you want to accentuate the positives in your body. And don't forget to wear colors that suit your complexion. All this is going to help you to feel more confident.

Make sure you feel comfortable in what you're wearing. You want to wear clothes that represent who you are. Be smart but relaxed. Do not wear clothes that distract you from connecting, like heels that are too high, a top that keeps coming off your shoulder, or a skirt or a shirt that's a little too tight. You also don't want to wear clothes that make you feel stiff or self-conscious. If you are going somewhere and you are not sure if the place has a dress code, don't be afraid to ask your date—he'll be happy to know that you are trying to look good for him.

When you are out with someone, make sure to compliment your date on something he is wearing or how he looks, as when people go on dates, they tend to put a lot of effort into looking good. So if you let your date know that you can tell he has put in effort, you will make him happy and score some points in the process.

32 Make Sure That You Are on the Same Page

Not everyone that dates has marriage on her mind. Many people just want to go on dates and are not ready to be with one person for the rest of their lives.

With that in mind, clarify for yourself what you want to get out of dating. Do you just want a social experience with different people? Do you want to have a serious relationship? Do you want to meet your life partner? Or are you just looking to get sexual experience?

Your goal will determine how you approach dating. If you had asked me what I wanted from dating at twenty-one, I would have said, "Experience," and if you had asked me at thirty-one, I would have said, "To meet my life partner." And if you are indeed ready to meet your life partner, then what is your goal? Be realistic. Do you see yourself married in the next three years? Five years? Ten years?

When you are clear about what you want out of dating, then you can be clear with the people that you are dating. If you just want to go out with a bunch of different people, then make it known to the person you are with that it is not your intention to commit yourself to any one person now. If your date is looking for her life partner, then do not lead her down a false path. Instead, do her a favor and don't waste her time. In the same vein, if you are looking for a life partner and the person you are on a date with is looking to casually date a number of people, then walk away. She is not for you, and if you wind up liking her, you could get hurt. Do not make the mistake of thinking that you can change her goal. However much you like your date, you are both at different places in your lives.

33 What NOT to Do on a First Date

Avoid these common dating missteps:

1. Don't drink too much on a first date. It's not very attractive to be with someone who is out of control or someone who seems to have a drinking problem. Also, if you are slightly off center from alcohol, it could make you do things you will regret later.

2. Don't talk about your ex, as it's not very attractive. Talking about your ex will make your current date think you are not over him or her. And besides, whatever you say will reveal more about you than it will about your ex, so it's better to say nothing.

3. Don't talk about yourself the whole time, especially not about anything too personal or having to do with your emotional problems.

4. Don't just push food around your plate. Make sure you eat if you are going out for dinner. When someone takes you out,

it's impolite to show little appreciation for the meal. Also, mind your table manners while you're at it!

5. Don't talk about marriage, commitment and/or having children.

6. Don't overdo the perfume or aftershave; you don't want to smell like a brothel. Make sure you are clean and let your natural scent come through.

7. Don't show off every part of your body. Leave something to the imagination when you get dressed. Wear something that is relaxed yet smart at the same time.

8. Don't lie. Lies will always catch up with you! Always tell the truth and don't try to be someone you are not.

9. Don't be late. You don't want to start your date by insulting or annoying the person you are meeting.

10. Don't have sex, unless you are interested only in a one-night stand. Retain a bit of mystery.

11. Don't let the date go on too long. Ideally, you really want to part at the peak, when you are having lots of fun, so that the joy doesn't get a chance to wane at all.

12. Don't answer your cell phone on a date. In fact, turn it off.

13. Don't be rude to the waiter.

14. Don't talk badly about anyone, whether they are strangers in the restaurant, a friend or family member.

15. Avoid self-deprecating comments about yourself or your body. Your date doesn't want to know if you wish you had better abs or are trying to lose weight.

34 What to Do on a Date

Here are some foolproof ways to make a good impression and have fun on a date:

1. Do keep the conversation positive.

2. Do maintain good eye contact, as that can be very attractive.

3. Do keep your body language open. If you are interested in the other person, this will happen naturally, anyway.

4. Do make sure to smile.

5. Do show that you have a sense of humor and laugh at your date's jokes. And if it feels natural and easy, you can crack some of your own!

6. Do know what is going on in the world so that you can show that you are interested and up to date on world affairs and culture.

7. Do compliment your date on something that he is wearing. Be honest and notice something that he obviously took time over.

8. Do enjoy yourself. Be easygoing, fun, go with the flow and find where you both connect.

9. Do something fun. There are plenty of activities to do on a first date apart from the obvious dinner and a movie. Here are a few ideas:

    Play tennis or another sport and chitchat while doing it.

    Go to the beach or countryside and have a picnic.

    Go rollerblading.

    Play mini golf or go for a hike.

    Go to a music festival or concert.

    Go to the theater or cabaret.

There are so many other activities, so do your best to think outside of the box.

35 Make Small Talk

Remember, ANYWHERE, ANYTIME. You could be in an airport, waiting to check out at the grocery store or running on a treadmill at the gym. Knowing this, you need to be confident enough to connect at any moment. What this means is that you need to become a master of small talk and get used to talking to people you don't know. If you know that you are quite shy, then it is best to practice with all different types of people to help yourself get over your shyness.

The number one way to connect with someone is to keep your senses open to what they are doing, what they are wearing, what they are eating. You want to connect with something about them and not about you. And you need to be genuinely interested. It takes confidence, but don't stress—people love to talk about themselves.

Be casual and relaxed with the other person. If she has a dog, ask her what his name is. If you are sitting next to someone on a train, discuss what he is reading. Connect!

Once you have a conversation going, maintain eye contact and keep your body language open. We are already unconscious masters of body language and flirting, and for many it comes easy, but for others it is more difficult. Flirting is about confidence.

Additionally, when you are on a date, you want to make sure that you always keep the conversation flowing. Small talk can really save you from the dreaded awkward silence.

Here are nine good questions to pose to someone after you've already struck up a conversation and developed a rapport, just in case you need some way to keep the conversation going:

1. What is your favorite hobby?

2. What is your favorite destination in the world that you've been to, and where would you most like to go that you haven't been?

3. If you could take up any new hobby, what would it be?

4. What are the things that you would love to do but are scared to?

5. Do you love your work, and if so, what do you love about it?

6. If you could pick another career and it could be anything that you want to do, what would you choose?

7. What are your top five favorite movies?

8. Which people, dead or alive, would you most like to invite for dinner?

9. If you could live anywhere in the world, where would it be?

Just remember to relax. And don't ask the questions like a firing squad, all at the same time! Pick one and allow the answer to lead your conversation in a new direction.

36 Follow These Tips for Internet Dating

Whenever I meet someone who is looking for a partner and is having difficulty, I always ask if he has looked into internet dating. Let's face it—it's easy, it's convenient and nowadays it seems like practically everyone is doing it. Give it a shot and keep the following tips in mind and you'll have nothing to lose.

Be Clear about What You Want

Before you even start looking for a date online, be really clear about why you are doing it and what you are looking for. If you are looking for a life partner, then choose a dating website that is geared toward people who are serious about finding a life partner. If you want to casually date, then choose a site that is set up specifically for that. There are so many different dating sites geared to so many different groups, and it pays to do the research to find one that really fits you and what you are looking for.

Pay for It

Make sure that you pay a monthly fee for the website access as fee-based sites attract like-minded people who are serious about finding a partner. Nobody likes to waste money!

Your Photo

Make sure you use a very recent photo of yourself in which you are smiling and looking approachable. It is ideal to use a photo that is head and shoulders, has good lighting and is in color. If you're forty, don't post a photo of you when you were twenty just because you look younger and thinner. The last thing you want to do is to meet someone and see the look of disappointment on his face because you essentially lied. In the same vein, you wouldn't want to meet someone who looks completely different than his photo, either.

Also, post only one photo, or two at the most, but no more. You want to leave something to the imagination. Make sure you are dressed in the photo the way you usually dress, rather than wearing something special that doesn't accurately represent the everyday you.

Your Profile

Take your profile very seriously. Treat it like a résumé, and get a friend who knows you well and a family member to check it over to see if they think it accurately describes you. Be honest about yourself. You want to be liked for who you *are,* not who you *are not* or who you want to be.

When you write about yourself, focus on what is unique about you, and remember to be specific. If you love learning languages, give an example (for example, I recently completed a six-month course in Mandarin). Or if you love animals, and you swam with wild dolphins last year in Costa Rica, say so in your profile. You want to describe your hobbies and qualities in terms of what you have done recently or would love to do. You are trying to capture someone's imagination so that person really gets a sense of you. Providing an example is much more powerful than just saying, "I love learning languages" or "I love animals."

Make sure you are positive in your profile. Don't be negative about past relationships or anything else you may write about. Keep your language clean, and don't talk about sex in your profile or when you start emailing someone. It can (and probably will) be considered creepy and crude. You will also find that it will be very ineffective in finding a serious long-term partner.

Finally, make sure that you are concise and clear about what you are looking for.

Making Contact

Before you email someone, make sure that you have really read his profile and everything that he says about himself so that you may properly connect with him. For instance, if you see that he is from New York and it is one of your favorite cities, New York could be a springboard for a discussion. If his favorite film is the same as yours, let him know to spark a conversation.

As well as emailing back and forth, you might want to speak to this person on the phone a few times before you meet. A voice says a lot about someone.

Also, try to find out about this person through other people or through the internet so you can clarify that he is who he says he is before you meet him.

Treat everyone that you are in communication with through email with the utmost respect. If you do meet someone you like and don't want to continue emailing anyone else that you have been in contact with, make it clear to those people that you have met someone. And be honest. Even though you are connecting in cyberspace, there is a person at the other end who has feelings, too. At the same time don't be disappointed if you like someone when you email, but it doesn't go any further.

The Meeting

Your first meeting should be in a public place, during the day, if possible. Meet for coffee, happy hour or even tapas so that you can spend as little as fifteen minutes together but can extend the meeting to two hours if you want to.

Do not be disappointed if you seemed to get along brilliantly in your email correspondence and on the phone but do not connect when you actually meet. Dating is a numbers game and so much has to do with the sight, sound and smell of the other person, with the face-to-face interaction.

Remember that there are many people out there, so don't be discouraged by rejection. Like always, just keep moving forward. There will be someone for you.

For safety reasons do not tell the person you are meeting exactly where you live, in case he is not who he says he is or turns out to be a stalker! Trust your instincts. If you feel that the person you are seeing seems unbalanced, then leave quickly.

Make sure you tell a friend or family member exactly where you are meeting your date. While I generally advise against using cell phones on a first date, in this instance it's best to make sure your friend or family member calls you early on in the meeting to check that you are okay. Give your friend or family member your date's name, online name and photo.

37 Find Out These 7 Essential Things about Your Date

When you are attracted to someone, it is easy to be bowled over by that person when he is on his best behavior and you have on rose-colored spectacles, so do your best to stay conscious and aware.

When you go on your first few dates with someone, there are things to look out for and you need to be a bit of a detective and listen to what isn't being said as much as you listen to what is said.

You don't want to ask your date so many questions that she feels as if she is in an interrogation room. But you need to keep your eyes and ears open and your senses aware. Try to determine the answers to the following seven questions.

1. **How close is your date to his or her family?**
    Find out about your date's family experience and how close he is to his parents. Does he talk to them a lot? Does he make time to see them? This will say a lot about whether he is a family person. Notice if his family is number one or if work seems to come first, because his priorities most likely will be the same when you are with him.

2. **Does your date like children?**
   Notice if your date mentions anything about kids. Does she have a nephew or niece she's nuts about, or does she hate being in places where there are kids screaming?

3. **How do your date's parents behave?**
   Do your date's mom and dad fight all the time? Do they have a tendency to continue arguments for weeks on end? Do these arguments ever get violent? Or do they refrain from talking and instead hide everything under the carpet?

   Oftentimes, the way people act in a relationship will mirror the relationship they observed between their parents, so this is always an important topic to pay attention to.

4. **What are your date's relationships like with others?**
   How are your date's relationships with friends, coworkers and siblings? Is he comfortable around other people? How does he speak to his parents? Is he respectful? Does he listen to other people when they talk?

5. **How well does your date mix with your friends and family?**
   You can tell a lot about someone by how they interact in a social situation with your friends and with your family. Do they all get along well or is it a bit strained? It is always good to get an opinion from the people who love you, as they have a bit of distance and will want the best for you.

6. **Is your date ambitious?**

   Does he achieve his goals easily? Is he driven? Is he really good at what he does? Does he love what he does?

7. **How does your date react in hard times?**

   The stories that your date tells you of how she reacted in hard times reveal a lot about her nature. They reveal how she reacts when life gets tough. When things get tough, does she resort to placing blame on external forces, or is she proactive, doing her best to keep herself afloat?

PART III

CREATING
LIFELONG LOVE

8 Fan the Small Flame

I remember going to a talk given by the spiritual teacher Ravi Shankar many years ago, and in the talk he said something that really struck me. He said when you meet someone and there is an immediate huge flame, it cannot grow as it is already at its full capacity. However, when you meet someone and there is a smaller flame, it can grow.

I took this to mean that a larger flame indicates less potential for long-term stability in a relationship. After all, a flame at its peak can only peter out from there. A smaller flame has the potential and space to grow over time—it may not be very bright at this moment, but it is steadier and more consistent and has the potential to become even brighter and to last much longer.

If you ask those who are in a really loving, stable marriage, many will likely tell you that the feelings they experienced when they met their spouse were unlike any that they felt in past relationships.

You need to keep your senses open, because the feelings you experience upon meeting someone might not be initially profound, especially if you're used to starting a relationship with huge sparks. Notice if you feel more comfortable with the person than you ever have with anyone before, and get a sense if there is an ease between you that feels unusual and if the person inspires you to be yourself and the best you can be. Everyone has a unique experience when they meet their partner; however, there is usually a real sense of having come home. Don't be so quick to write things off if you aren't blown over by someone initially or if huge fireworks don't happen right away. Remember that if your relationship is different from all the other relationships that have come before, then you may be onto something special. Your ultimate goal is not to *fall* in love. It is to *grow* in love.

39 Mind the Third Person in Your Relationship

When two people come together, a dynamic is created that is half you and half your partner. It is like a new person is created, a third person, who has both of your strengths and weaknesses and all of your personality traits combined.

With that in mind, realize that whatever your last partner was like, you helped to bring out those qualities and highlight them. The expression of that relationship was your combined dynamic.

I remember feeling very slighted in one of my long-term relationships because I felt that my boyfriend wasn't passionate enough. So I used to criticize him as a way for me to retain power and not take responsibility. As time went on, I realized I had two choices: I could keep this story going, analyze it "till the cows came home" and remain a "victim," or I could look at how I had a part in it and accept that our combined dynamic just wasn't that passionate and that there was something in me that was attracting someone who was physically unavailable. Ultimately I realized that it wasn't his fault and it wasn't mine; it was just the joint dynamic that had been created between us that did not work.

40 Discover Your Sexual Compatibility

Sexual compatibility is a very important thing for a strong, healthy relationship. There is no right or wrong amount of sex to have and every couple is totally different. The only thing that matters is that you and your partner are both in agreement over your sexual frequency and compatibility.

It would be ideal to find someone who has a similar sexual appetite to yours; however, this is generally not the sort of topic that comes up halfway through the first date. If you both want and need different amounts of sex, it is important to talk about it while you are still dating, as it is unlikely to change when you get married. If you think you can dovetail what you both need, then great. If not, then your incompatibility is not going to change.

If you believe that you are with your life partner and really want to make it work, but there is a discrepancy in what you both desire, then discuss your needs and what you can do to make each other happy. Make it work before you tie the knot, because when you do get married, you are essentially saying, *"I am happy to exist like this for the rest of my life."*

41 Be Clear on Money Issues

- -

When you marry someone, you also marry his or her bank account! Be clear with your partner about how you deal with money so that you avoid potential pitfalls later on. If you are someone who saves and has no debts and your partner is someone who spends and has lots of debts, then it's best to come to some agreements on money before you tie the knot.

I, for instance, am a saver. I like to live within my means and I am quite prudent with money when it is tight. When I feel that there is not enough money coming into the house, then I start to get something called Bag-Lady Syndrome. It seems that a number of women develop this syndrome, regardless of their financial status, which is the fear of being left out on the street, homeless and penniless.

My husband, on the other hand, is naturally more of a spender. He has learned to save through more difficult times, but we really do have different ideas about money, which we most likely gleaned from our different upbringings.

Discussing money can cause all sorts of emotions depending on how you were brought up to view it. Think about your parents'

attitudes toward money. Did they think that if you worked hard, you would make money? Did they think that money was easy to come by?

For some reason it is considered rude to ask anyone how much money they earn. In fact, it is probably considered more rude than asking about their sex life! But you need to develop your own healthy money habits, and if you do that, you are more likely to attract someone who has healthy habits as well.

Here are some questions for you to answer with your partner:

1. Are you a spender or a saver?

2. Do you have debt? If so, how much?

3. What are your financial goals for one year, five years, ten years and thirty years from now?

4. What is your family's attitude toward money?

5. Are you realistic about money?

6. Are you organized with money?

7. Are you generous with money?

8. Do you find it easy to make money?

9. Do you find it easy to discuss money?

10. What issues involving money are you unclear about?

42 Look at a Potential Partner's Relationship History

If you meet someone you just aren't quite sure about, try to pry ever so slightly into their relationship history. If you come to realize that this person has been with many other perfectly lovely companions but has never been able to hold down a long-term relationship, keep in mind that it is unlikely that he will be able to in the near future. (There are exceptionally rare cases where someone thinks it's a waste of time to be in a relationship long term and get emotionally attached unless it is with a life partner—but trust me, these cases are few and far between.)

However, these cases do exist. Before I met my husband, he had not been in a proper long-term relationship in the ten years before we started dating, just because he thought it was a waste of time. I am saying this to show that there are always exceptions to the rule!

Here are some questions you can ask yourself to gauge someone's ability to commit:

1. Does he have a stable career, or does he switch jobs all the time?

2. Does she move every year or stay put?

3. Does he have a pet he takes care of?

4. Does she have a plant that she actually waters?

5. Does he have a lot of old close friends, or did he meet his best friend six months ago?

6. Are her close friends married, or are they all still single?

43 Connect Through Vulnerability

We are all vulnerable. And when we meet someone new, we are usually at our most vulnerable. Connecting through vulnerability doesn't mean that you can't be strong and self-confident. It just means that being warm, considerate and open are extremely important, too.

Appearing completely perfect or giving the impression that you have it all figured out is not a great dating strategy, as it can make the other person feel that you don't need him at all and there is no place for him to fit in and no way to connect with you. In general, we tend to bond with others through our vulnerability, rather than through pretending that we are completely perfect. Of course, you don't want to go on a date and immediately begin to discuss your problems, but you also don't want to appear as if you have it all together without any room left to grow.

The important thing to keep in mind is the idea of being open and letting yourself be vulnerable to another person. When you embrace this honest way of being, you are bound to convey this openness with your body language and attitude, too.

44 Understand How Men and Women Communicate Differently

Men and women are wired differently and, as a result, communicate in different ways. It helps to understand this so that you can better communicate with your partner and also understand why you need strong friendships outside of your relationship to fulfill certain needs that your partner cannot.

Understanding how men and women communicate differently will help you to become more patient and accepting and will also clarify that no one person is able to give you everything that you need. He is not supposed to and you don't want him to.

Women love deep, meaningful conversations and understand life through their interactions with others and are good at such exchanges. We connect our emotions with language and try to establish a certain kind of intimacy by sharing with each other what is on our mind or what we have been up to. We chat about how events have an emotional effect on us, and discussing it with a friend is a way of releasing stress, without necessarily looking for solutions. By connecting with the other person, we feel vital and alive and are showing them that we trust them.

The majority of men find it hard to communicate how they feel through words, so they are not great sharers. They are much better at showing how they feel through actions. If you see a bunch of guys together, they are usually talking about events and activities, not about feelings. Men tend to connect by doing activities together. So watch what a man does rather than what he says, because you will understand how a man feels through watching his actions. Does he make you dinner? Does he rub your feet? Does he buy you flowers? If everything was mute and you just watched him as you would a silent film, would you see actions of love? Even if you are the kind of person who is full of sweet nothings, don't expect your man to reciprocate with words.

Women talk about what is on their mind to release stress, but men talk about their problems to find a solution. This difference can frustrate many couples, as a woman might feel that she's not being heard if her boyfriend tries to "fix" her problems instead of listening empathetically, and a man doesn't understand why his girlfriend doesn't listen to his advice, when the truth is that she just wants to talk about it.

Ordinarily a man will withdraw to work out his own problems, rather than discuss them with a woman. He might talk about them once he has worked them out himself, so as a woman you need to let him withdraw to figure things out by himself. If you want to help, buy him a six-pack or his favorite cookies to take to his cave and wait for him to emerge as the conquering hero when he has come up with his own solution.

Women must keep these differences in mind and know that if they need a good, long intense chat, it is wise to call a girlfriend. They must not try to turn their partner into one.

Men also need to understand that when a woman is talking, her underlying motivation is to create intimacy with him, regardless of how important he thinks the subject is that she is discussing. So if a man can share a bit more of himself with his woman by chatting with her in an intimate way and listening to her, then she will be getting some of her needs met and she will feel loved by him.

No matter how great their relationship is with a man, women need to chat with their girlfriends, and no matter how great a man's relationship is with his girlfriend, he needs to go and hang out with his male friends. Recognizing that you both have different needs that the other cannot fulfill will ultimately make for a healthy relationship.

45 Praise and Appreciate Your Partner

Always let your partner know how much you appreciate what he does for you. Let him know the ways in which he makes you happy. Tell him how great he is in bed. Let him know how attractive you think he is, how much you respect him and what he does for a living. Your partner can't guess what's on your mind, and he wants to know that he is all you need. Also, show him how grateful you are for his generosity as much as you possibly can through actions. Perhaps do an errand for him, butter his toast, massage his shoulders or buy him his favorite chocolates. It's the little things that you do to show you have noticed his generosity that make a big difference.

If you are ever in the situation in which your partner says, "I feel that I can never make you happy," then you are not offering him enough praise or showing him enough appreciation for him to know that he is making you happy. This is a sign that if you are not careful, he will look for someone else who will be happy with him and what he can provide. So be sure to show your thanks through words and actions all the time.

46 Be a Good Listener

The most appealing thing you can do on a date is to listen to the other person. Do not pretend you are listening, but actively listen so that the other person feels heard and understood.

Active listening means that you devote your full attention to your date and genuinely care what she is saying and encourage her to keep talking. People love to be listened to attentively, and they can tell if you are half listening or organizing your thoughts when they are speaking and if you are much more interested in having your say than letting them speak.

I have heard many people say that Bill Clinton is a great example of an active listener. People who have met him say that when you talk to him, it is like you are the only person there. He never looks around; he looks you in the eye and he is completely and utterly engaged in what you are saying. You need to be like that on a date, and you also need to keep your eyes peeled as to whether your date is fully engaged or seems to only be half listening. If he or she has a wandering eye or mind the first few times you are together, this will likely be an issue further down the line.

47 Avoid These 7 Red Flags

You will never love everything about someone, but you need to know what your deal breakers are. Start with these red flags and you may also be inspired to add some of your own.

1. **Jealous:** If you are with someone who has a tendency to get jealous, you won't feel free to be yourself in the relationship, especially if you get along well with people of the gender you date. Even if you think that this jealous behavior is rather cute and flattering at first, someone controlling what you do, where you go or who you see will make you feel very stifled in the long run.

2. **Abusive:** If he is physically or verbally abusive, makes disparaging comments and is rude, run like the wind in the opposite direction and never look back.

3. **Addicted:** If she is addicted to alcohol, drugs, gambling, food or anything else, the addiction is ultimately going to take preference over you. It is unlikely your partner will love you more than she loves the addiction and you will have to live with it as well.

4. **Deceitful:** If your partner is really dishonest and has problems with lying, you will never be able to fully trust him.

5. **Disloyal:** If your partner has a history of being disloyal, she may betray your trust.

6. **Taken:** If your partner is not really single, even though he says he is and insists that his relationship is falling apart, it is likely that you will remain the one kept on the side.

7. **Unavailable:** If your partner isn't there when you need her most at the beginning, she won't be there later on.

48 How to Recognize if They Like You

Wondering if the relationship is working? Here are some signs:

1. **Family Matters:** He asks you to meet his family. It means that you are not just passing in and out of his life. It is a good sign if he invites you to big family occasions; for example, a wedding or his grandmother's ninetieth birthday.

2. **Thinking of You:** He thinks about you and remembers things you say and buys you gifts out of the blue. He compliments you on who you are as a person, rather than on how you look.

3. **The Future:** He plans vacations and other events with you months in advance. He talks about what he wants in the future and asks you what your vision is.

4. **Making Contact:** He calls/emails/texts you regularly. He assumes that you are going to be together each weekend.

49 Every Cell Has to Scream, "Yes! Yes! Yes!"

Do not even think of marrying unless every cell in your body screams, "Yes, this is the person for me! This is the person that I want to go through thick and thin with!"

Do NOT consider marriage if you don't feel 100 percent sure about the relationship. This doesn't mean your partner has to be 100 percent perfect, as that is not possible. He isn't; you aren't! But you have to feel that together, as a team, you have the basis of a really strong, stable, loyal relationship and that you will support each other to heal and grow through good times and tough times. If even a tiny bit of you is doubtful, then don't get married and either wait until you do feel 100 percent sure or move on! Because that little voice of doubt can become louder and louder over time, until you can't hear anything else or wish you had listened in the first place.

When I met my husband, I knew almost instantly that my relationship with him was going to be different. For the first time the little voice of doubt was absent. When I walked up the aisle to marry my husband, every cell in my body knew that he was the man for me.

50 Have Faith in Timing

Meeting your life partner is not just about you taking steps; it is also about your life partner taking steps. And since you haven't met him yet (or perhaps you have but don't know it), you have no control over his development.

Every tip in this book is designed to make *you* ready, to get you to a place where you are whole and complete and feeling fully happy with who you are. Then it is a matter of waiting for everything to line up so that you two do come together. Timing is key!

In the Introduction, I told you how I met my husband, Oli, out of the blue. In a similar way you may notice when you look back after meeting the person you are going to marry that your encounter happened out of nowhere, when meeting someone was not at the forefront of your mind and you were perhaps looking in the other direction. You have control of your own path, so work on that, one step at a time. Trust that there is someone out there for you and it will happen—you will meet your ideal mate—and in the meantime keep working on yourself to strip away old unworkable habits and beliefs so that you can mag-netize someone who likes you for who you are.

ANYWHERE. ANYTIME.

One day you are single; the next you are with your life part-ner. So hold on to your vision of what you want, and trust that it will happen to you as it has happened and continues to happen every day to so many other people, no matter what their age or circumstance, and remember to have fun along the way!

SO, HOW HAPPY *IS* YOUR LOVE LIFE?

Now it's time to find out how happy your love life really is—and how you can make it even happier. Take your quiz responses and follow the suggestions below to see which tips are best for you as you search for true love.

1. **If you answered:**
    A. See tips: 2, 4, 6, 7, 8, 10, 11, 12, 13, 14, 18, 19, 22, 23, 25, 26, 30, 50
    B. See tips: 2, 3, 4, 6, 7, 8, 10, 11, 12, 14, 18, 22, 25, 26, 50
    C. You learn from all your past experiences so that you can have a healthier, more successful relationship next time. Now read on for additional tips to make your love life even happier.

2. **If you answered:**
    A. See tips: 1, 12, 15, 16, 18, 19, 25, 26, 30
    B. See tips: 1, 2, 3, 4, 5, 6, 8, 9, 10, 11, 12, 13, 14, 15, 16, 17, 18, 19, 21, 22, 24, 25, 26, 30, 43, 50
    C. You seem to have a healthy attitude about finding love and trust that there is someone out there for you. Now read on for additional tips to make your love life even happier.

3. **If you answered:**
   A. See tips: 2, 3, 4, 6, 7, 12, 14, 16, 18, 23, 37, 39, 42, 43, 47, 48
   B. See tips: 12, 16, 18, 24
   C. See tips: 2, 4, 6, 12, 15, 16, 18, 22, 24, 37, 42, 43

4. **If you answered:**
   A. See tips: 1, 2, 4, 6, 7, 9, 12, 13, 15, 16, 17, 18, 19, 22, 25, 26, 37, 47, 49, 50
   B. You are making the most of your life. Now read on for additional tips to make your love life even happier.
   C. See tips: 2, 3, 4, 6, 7, 9, 11, 12, 13, 14, 15, 16, 17, 18, 37, 47, 49, 50

5. **If you answered:**
   A. See tips: 2, 4, 6, 7, 8, 10, 11, 12, 15, 16, 18, 43, 44, 46
   B. It's very healthy to address your issues head-on. This will make your next relationship that much healthier. Now read on for additional tips to make your love life even happier.
   C. See tips: 2, 3, 4, 6, 7, 10

6. **If you answered:**
   A. See tips: 1, 2, 4, 6, 7, 8, 9, 10, 11, 12, 14, 16, 18, 19, 22, 23, 24, 25, 26, 28
   B. See tips: 2, 4, 8
   C. See tips: 1, 2, 4, 6, 7, 8, 9, 10, 11, 12, 13, 14, 15, 16, 17, 18, 19, 21, 22, 24, 25, 26, 28, 30, 32, 33, 34, 36, 37, 38, 44, 45, 46, 47

7. **If you answered:**
   A. See tips: 4, 6, 12, 16, 22, 23, 24, 41, 47
   B. You listen to your family but at the same time trust your own instincts above all. Now read on for additional tips to make your love life even happier.
   C. See tips: 4, 23, 32, 37, 41, 42, 47

8. **If you answered:**
   A. See tip: 40
   B. See tips: 23, 39, 40, 43, 49
   C. See tips: 23, 39, 40, 49

9. **If you answered:**
   A. See tips: 33, 37

   B. You are being sensible by being patient and allowing the relationship to grow and evolve without pushing it. Now read on for additional tips to make your love life even happier.

   C. See tips: 3, 34, 37, 43

10. **If you answered:**
    A. You know that while you may not have a partner to share the holidays with now, you will someday. Now read on for additional tips to make your love life even happier.

    B. See tips: 1, 2, 4, 6, 7, 8, 9, 11, 12, 13, 14, 15, 16, 17, 18, 19, 50

    C. See tips: 1, 2, 4, 6, 12, 14, 17, 18, 19, 50

11. **If you answered:**
    A. See tips: 2, 4, 6, 8, 12, 15, 16, 18, 22, 24

    B. By spending time to determine what you want in a partner, you'll be able to recognize when he or she comes along! Now read on for additional tips to make your love life even happier.

    C. See tips: 2, 4, 6, 8, 12, 16, 18, 22, 23, 24, 37

12. **If you answered:**
    A. See tips: 2, 5, 6, 7, 12, 14, 15, 16, 18, 22
    B. See tips: 2, 6, 12, 15, 16, 18, 22, 37
    C. You are surrounding yourself with relationships that work so that you too can magnetize a great working love relationship into your life. Now read on for additional tips to make your love life even happier.

13. **If you answered:**
    A. See tips: 2, 7, 10, 12, 15, 17, 18, 30, 33, 34, 35, 36, 37, 44, 46, 47, 48, 50
    B. See tips: 17, 30, 34, 35, 36, 37, 46, 47
    C. You know that by getting out there you are increasing your chances of meeting the *one*. Now read on for additional tips to make your love life even happier.

14. **If you answered:**
    A. See tips: 2, 9, 12, 17, 18, 25, 26, 33, 34, 35, 36
    B. By going to new places and trying new things, you're opening yourself up to many more possibilities. Now read on for additional tips to make your love life even happier.
    C. See tips: 2, 4, 6, 8, 11, 12, 15, 16, 17, 18, 25, 26, 34, 35, 36

15. If you answered:

   A. See tips: 21, 22, 23, 24, 37, 44, 47

   B. See tips: 2, 4, 6, 7, 9, 12, 16, 18, 19, 22, 23, 24, 32, 37

   C. You are smart enough to know that no one is perfect. Now read on for additional tips to make your love life even happier.

16. If you answered:

   A. See tips: 2, 3, 4, 5, 6, 7, 8, 10, 11, 12, 14, 15, 16, 18, 19, 22, 23, 24, 25, 26, 28, 32, 37, 39, 42, 44, 45, 46, 47, 48, 50

   B. See tips: 2, 4, 6, 7, 8, 10, 12, 16, 18, 22, 23, 25, 26, 32, 37, 47

   C. See tips: 2, 4, 6, 7, 8, 10, 11, 12, 14, 15, 16, 18, 19, 22, 23, 24, 25, 26, 28, 37, 39, 40, 41, 42, 43, 44, 45, 46, 47, 48

17. If you answered:

   A. See tips: 2, 4, 6, 8, 10, 11, 12, 13, 14, 15, 16, 18, 22, 47, 49

   B. See tips: 22, 37, 43, 47

   C. It's important to pay attention to red flags and to address your concerns before deciding that it won't work out. Now read on for additional tips to make your love life even happier.

18. **If you answered:**

   A. You want to look nice and at the same time you know that it's important that you present your true self. Now read on for additional tips to make your love life even happier.

   B. See tips: 2, 4, 14, 28, 31, 33, 34

   C. See tips: 7, 12, 14, 18, 24, 29, 31, 33

19. **If you answered:**

   A. It makes no sense to start a relationship unless you both are mentally, emotionally and physically available. Now read on for additional tips to make your love life even happier.

   B. See tips: 2, 4, 6, 7, 12, 16, 18, 23, 24, 27, 32, 37, 42, 47

   C. See tips: 2, 4, 6, 7, 12, 14, 15, 16, 18, 19, 23, 24, 32, 42, 47

20. **If you answered:**

   A. See tips: 2, 4, 6, 7, 9, 11, 12, 14, 15, 16, 18, 19, 21, 24, 25, 26, 31, 32, 33, 34, 35, 37, 46, 47

   B. See tips: 2, 4, 7, 10, 11, 12, 16, 18, 24, 25, 26, 27, 28, 37, 38, 39, 42, 43, 44, 46, 47, 48

   C. See tips: 1, 2, 4, 6, 7, 9, 10, 11, 12, 16, 18, 25, 26, 37, 47

21. If you answered:
   A. See tips: 7, 9, 12, 18, 20, 34, 35, 37, 46, 47, 48

   B. See tips: 7, 9, 12, 18, 20, 34, 35, 37, 46, 47, 48

   C. You are observant and intuitive and can easily recognize when someone is interested in you. Now read on for additional tips to make your love life even happier.

22. If you answered:
   A. See tips: 28, 33, 37, 47, 48

   B. See tips: 8, 37, 42, 43, 47, 48

   C. You already know that it's important to be emotionally ready before you become physically intimate. Now read on for additional tips to make your love life even happier.

23. If you answered:
   A. See tips: 24, 37, 41, 42

   B. See tips: 23, 37, 41, 42

   C. See tips: 4, 23, 37, 41, 42

24. If you answered:

A. As far as your physical space is concerned, you're ready to make room for new love! Now read on for additional tips to make your love life even happier.

B. See tips: 2, 3, 7, 11, 12, 18, 25, 26, 32, 37, 43, 48

C. See tips: 2, 3, 4, 6, 7, 10, 11, 12, 15, 18, 22, 25, 26, 37, 48

25. If you answered:

A. See tips: 12, 23, 24, 39, 40, 41, 44, 45, 47, 49

B. You are going to make sure that every cell in your body screams, "Yes," before you make a lifelong commitment. Now read on for additional tips to make your love life even happier.

C. See tips: 23, 39, 40, 44, 47, 49

ACKNOWLEDGMENTS

I would like to thank the countless wonderful therapists, self-development trainers, life coaches and body workers who have in one way or another contributed to this book. From my early teens, each one of you has assisted me in peeling back my masks and armor to reveal my authentic self, which has helped focus my energies on making a difference. I would like to extend a special public thanks to Suzanne Campbell, Tony Wiseman, John Davis, Rita Homritch, Dr. Tom, Bill Cumming and Mike Robinson.

Thank you to my exceptional editor, Sarah Pelz, and the rest of the team at Harlequin, including Tara Kelly, Mark Tang and Shara Alexander.

I would like to express my gratitude to my fantastic literary agents, Shannon Marven and Lacy Lynch, and everyone at Dupree Miller. Thank you for pulling my book proposal out of the slush pile twice! It was obviously meant to be and proves that every now and again cold-calling can work!

Thanks are due to the *Huffington Post,* Joel Mandel, Scott Warren and KTLA. To Sam Fischer and P.J. Shapiro for watching my back, and Ashley Davis and Andrea Ross at CAA for being part of the team.

Thanks to my colleagues at HowHappyIs.com, especially our very gifted creative partner Jon Stout, and to Terri Carey for keeping us organized.

To my brother Nick for knowing Oli, to Marcel for being such a great friend and letting me stay in your house long enough so I could meet Oli, to Leanne for walking out of your house at the exact same time as Oli and to Hazel for inviting Oli for tea.

Thanks also go to Leanne Benjamin, Heidi Rose Robbins, Nina and Mike Neill, Renata Danobeitia and David Fraser for being soul mates along the way.

Oli, you are the love of my life. Judah, the happiest boy, you rock!

Look for these other books in the *How Happy Is* series!

**How Happy Is
Your Marriage?**

**How Happy Is
Your Home?**

**How Happy Is
Your Health?**